ELEANOR & MARY ALICE

PETA TAIT

CURRENCY PRESS
The performing arts publisher
www.currency.com.au

CURRENT THEATRE SERIES

First published in 2018
by Currency Press Pty Ltd,
PO Box 2287, Strawberry Hills, NSW, 2012, Australia
enquiries@currency.com.au
www.currency.com.au

in association with The Evatt Foundation and Tashmadada Theatre

Copyright: *Eleanor and Mary Alice* © Peta Tait, 2018.

COPYING FOR EDUCATIONAL PURPOSES

The Australian *Copyright Act 1968* (Act) allows a maximum of one chapter or 10% of this book, whichever is the greater, to be copied by any educational institution for its educational purposes provided that that educational institution (or the body that administers it) has given a remuneration notice to Copyright Agency (CA) under the Act.
For details of the CA licence for educational institutions contact CA, 11/66 Goulburn Street, Sydney, NSW, 2000; tel: within Australia 1800 066 844 toll free; outside Australia 61 2 9394 7600; fax: 61 2 9394 7601; email: info@copyright.com.au

COPYING FOR OTHER PURPOSES

Except as permitted under the Act, for example a fair dealing for the purposes of study, research, criticism or review, no part of this book may be reproduced, stored in a retrieval system, or transmitted in any form or by any means without prior written permission. All enquiries should be made to the publisher at the address above.

Any performance or public reading of *Eleanor and Mary Alice* is forbidden unless a licence has been received from the author or the author's agent. The purchase of this book in no way gives the purchaser the right to perform the play in public, whether by means of a staged production or a reading. All applications for public performance should be addressed to the author c/- Currency Press.

Typeset by Dean Nottle for Currency Press.
Cover features Mary Alice Evatt, 'Portrait of Moya Dyring (in a French town)', c.1938, 2008.174, Collection: Art Gallery of Ballarat. ©Rosalind Carrodus.
Cover design by Katy Wall.

Currency Press acknowledges the Traditional Owners of the Country on which we live and work. We pay our respects to all Aboriginal and Torres Strait Islander Elders, past and present.

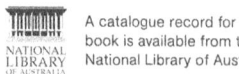
A catalogue record for this book is available from the National Library of Australia

Contents

ELEANOR AND MARY ALICE

    Act One   1

    Act Two   20

Theatre Program at the end of the playtext

ACKNOWLEDGEMENTS

Deborah Leiser-Moore and Peta Tait would like to thank all those who have supported this production over a number of years. We would especially like to thank Melissa Boyde, Meredith Rogers, Glenda Linscott, Richard Moore, Laura Sheedy, Heide Museum of Modern Art, Perth Centre for Photography, and the Board of The Evatt Foundation and in particular, Dr Chris Sheil, and staff at the Seymour Centre. We thank Professor Jane Lydon, Wesfarmers Chair of Australian History, University of Western Australia, for her invaluable support in 2016.

A special thank you to Rosalind Carrodus for permission to use Mary Alice Evatt's painting of Moya Dyring on the cover of this publication.

Thank you to Claire Grady, Katie Pollock and Currency Press.

Eleanor and Mary Alice was first produced by The Evatt Foundation and Tashmadada at the Seymour Centre, Sydney, on 5 December 2018, with the following cast:

ELEANOR ROOSEVELT	Sarah McNeill
MARY ALICE EVATT	Petra Kalive
MUSICIAN (cello)	Adi Sappir
Recorded voices of:	
WINSTON CHURCHILL	
FRANKLIN D. ROOSEVELT	
DR HERBERT VERE EVATT	Richard Moore

Director, Deborah Leiser-Moore
Music, Adi Sappir (live cello music throughout)

Eleanor and Mary Alice is about war, human rights and art, and the personal worlds of the influential Eleanor Roosevelt and artist, Mary Alice Evatt. Eleanor visits Australia in 1943, flying across the Japanese patrolled Pacific, and wants Mary Alice to help her fly on to the battlefront. The two women meet again in Paris in 1948 when Eleanor is chairing the UN Committee developing the Universal Declaration of Human Rights and Dr Herbert Evatt is the first President of the UN General Assembly. Mary Alice has to be a peace-maker between Eleanor and Herbert. The play features Winston Churchill, Franklin D. Roosevelt and Herbert Evatt and verbatim comments.

A production of *Eleanor and Mary Alice* premiered, as a 55-minute version for an art gallery space, at Heide Museum of Modern Art, on 25 October 2014, with the following cast:

ELEANOR ROOSEVELT	Glenda Linscott
MARY ALICE EVATT	Petra Kalive
MUSICIAN (cello)	Adi Sappir
Recorded voices of:	
WINSTON CHURCHILL	
FRANKLIN D. ROOSEVELT	
DR HERBERT VERE EVATT	Richard Moore

Director, Deborah Leiser Moore
Sound, Richard Moore
Music, Adi Sappir

Eleanor and Mary Alice was restaged at the Perth Centre for Photography in conjunction with the Human Rights Exhibition Project, Visualising Universalism, Perth, WA, on 8–11 December, 2016. It was performed in the midst of the remounted 1950–4 touring exhibition that presented the original Universal Declaration of Human Rights document. Sarah McNeill played Eleanor.

CHARACTERS

ELEANOR ROOSEVELT

MARY ALICE EVATT

WINSTON CHURCHILL

FRANKLIN D. ROOSEVELT

DR HERBERT VERE EVATT

A play for two or three actors.

Scenes with Churchill, Roosevelt and Evatt can be performed live by the third actor or recorded.

SETTING

Act One could be a domestic interior or an art studio with paintings.

Act Two could be a bench in the garden in front of the Palais de Chaillot or a French café.

PRODUCTION NOTES

There can be music (cello or jazz) in the background. There could be the sound of a fountain in Act Two.

The play can be performed in a theatre or a gallery space.

This is a flexible play text. Scenes with Churchill, Roosevelt and Evatt can be used selectively.

This play went to press before the end of rehearsals and may differ from the play as performed.

ACT ONE

SCENE ONE

ELEANOR ROOSEVELT *and* MARY ALICE EVATT.
Canberra, 4 September 1943 (World War II).

MARY ALICE: I am very, very pleased you've come, Mrs Roosevelt.
ELEANOR: You are the only one who is pleased, Mrs Evatt, the only one. The American generals are displeased.
MARY ALICE: There might be some puzzled Australian officials at this very moment.
ELEANOR: Have you been told *not* to let me out of your sight?
MARY ALICE: Well …
ELEANOR: Thank you for rescuing me.
MARY ALICE: I hear that you are good at evading officials yourself.
ELEANOR: Not as good as I'd like to be.
MARY ALICE: I longed to get away when we visited America last year.
ELEANOR: Protocol is relentless.
MARY ALICE: Let's dispense with it. I want to introduce you to someone.
ELEANOR: [*sighing*] A political campaigner?
MARY ALICE: An artist.
ELEANOR: [*relieved, looking around*] I'm happy to talk to an artist.
MARY ALICE: Her paintings. She left to live in Paris. I want you to meet Moya Dyring.
ELEANOR: Is she in Paris now during this war?

Pause.

MARY ALICE: No. I'm worried … about her health.
ELEANOR: We live for news.
MARY ALICE: Silence is painful.
ELEANOR: I did want this opportunity to have a private conversation.
MARY ALICE: With me?
ELEANOR: I need advice …
MARY ALICE: I'm not sure I'm the best person …

ELEANOR: A wife's perspective. I'm sure Mr Evatt confides in you about foreign affairs.
MARY ALICE: [*reluctantly agreeing*] At times.
ELEANOR: I need support for my change of schedule.
MARY ALICE: Is it unofficial?
ELEANOR: Franklin wanted me to do this visit.
MARY ALICE: Do we have a choice in wartime?
ELEANOR: I doubt that these trips have any real value right now—
MARY ALICE: That's not so.
ELEANOR: —or at any time?
MARY ALICE: Your visit is important.
ELEANOR: I can't see the public good from my visit.
MARY ALICE: You're an example.
ELEANOR: The attention on me takes away from the war effort.
MARY ALICE: We all feel helpless with all those poor young men … dying …
ELEANOR: To be honest, I've been dreading these thirteen days in Australia.
MARY ALICE: [*surprised*] But you have us here, Bert and myself.
ELEANOR: I feel I'm a nuisance.
MARY ALICE: Not to us!
ELEANOR: The pomp and the military police escort. The royalty business is excessive.
MARY ALICE: The crowds flock to see the most famous American woman.
ELEANOR: I'm a curiosity.
MARY ALICE: They won't believe that you've flown across the Pacific to Australia in the middle of the war unless they can see you for themselves.
ELEANOR: What good does it do?
MARY ALICE: Listen. Your visit shows that Australia is no longer cut off by this war. It's hopeful.
ELEANOR: I have to do much more than shake hands to make it worthwhile.

> *Pause.*

MARY ALICE: What more can you do?
ELEANOR: [*an ironic tone*] A good wife benefits her husband's interests.
MARY ALICE: A wife should have her own.

ACT ONE

ELEANOR: But his come first.
MARY ALICE: Ah, the life of a politician's wife, Mrs Roosevelt!
ELEANOR: Eleanor, please.
MARY ALICE: Mary Alice.

    Pause.

ELEANOR: I never had ambitions, Mary Alice. Fate has given me opportunities.
MARY ALICE: Yes, Mrs … Eleanor, in unexpected ways.
ELEANOR: On your visit to America before the war, you said public addresses and typing letters had taken over.
MARY ALICE: I did not expect to answer *all* his letters.
ELEANOR: I suppose this trip, this terrible chore, does give me a break from my husband's critics.
MARY ALICE: I can tell that you're tired. It's a very, very long flight. And getting on and off seventeen islands.
ELEANOR: The critics find me a soft target …

SCENE TWO

FRANKLIN ROOSEVELT.

December 1940.

ROOSEVELT: [*spoken live or recorded*] I am supporting a new lend-lease arrangement in which payment from an allied country for American planes and supplies is deferred for the duration of the war. But I envisage broader terms than monetary recompense. I want the agreement to include a clause about the allies working towards a fairer economic world for everyone after the war.

SCENE THREE

ELEANOR *and* MARY ALICE.

They are viewing a painting by Moya Dyring.

MARY ALICE: Does it swing?
ELEANOR: [*speaking slowly*] Swing is probably not a word I'd choose.
MARY ALICE: I picked it up in Paris before the war.
ELEANOR: How do I recognise if an image … swings?

MARY ALICE: Can you see action?
ELEANOR: I see people.
MARY ALICE: She's very good.
ELEANOR: I trust your judgment, Mary Alice.

Pause.

Why do you like art?
MARY ALICE: I love the world of shape and colour. I mean, I love my husband, my two children, but this invigorates me. I can't resist this demanding, never-ending puzzle over form.
ELEANOR: Can I see if your art ... swings?

Pause.

MARY ALICE: I'm not sure that's possible.
ELEANOR: Why not?
MARY ALICE: This is the only spare couple of hours in your schedule. You fly to Melbourne at eleven tomorrow.
ELEANOR: You refuse my small request after I've flown twenty-five thousand miles across Japanese-patrolled ocean?
MARY ALICE: [*smiling*] I'm flattered. I didn't realise you'd flown all the way across the Pacific to see my paintings.

ELEANOR *giggles slightly.*

ELEANOR: It's my secret mission for 1943. Don't tell the generals.
MARY ALICE: Next trip.
ELEANOR: Are you worried I'll write about you in my newspaper column?
MARY ALICE: Do you write about modern art?
ELEANOR: I write about what interests me.
MARY ALICE: I shall interest you in Moya's art. She follows Picasso and I follow her.
ELEANOR: It's clearly ... modern.
MARY ALICE: Why not cover artists in your column?
ELEANOR: If I describe how their work swings, my readers would desert me. Do you promote modern art to everyone?
MARY ALICE: It helps us see and feel ... differently.
ELEANOR: [*speaking slowly*] Are you showing me that Australia is modern and therefore should be defended by America?
MARY ALICE: [*smiling*] I'm simply showing you art by a friend.

ELEANOR: [*smiling*] The American command here does not ask for my opinion, you know.
MARY ALICE: You tell your husband everything.
ELEANOR: I did write Franklin that I like your Prime Minister Curtin.
MARY ALICE: Will you tell FDR … Franklin, about Moya?
ELEANOR: I can't really tell anyone about an exhibition.
MARY ALICE: You would seem to be wasting time?
ELEANOR: [*sighing*] As the President's wife, I'm only really expected to supervise the catering. There's one side benefit to this trip. I made sure Churchill had the food he likes for several weeks and walked out the next day leaving behind all the disruption.
MARY ALICE: Roast beef and cauliflower?
ELEANOR: [*smiling*] He eats some American food.

   Pause.

MARY ALICE: Is Churchill less rude to you at your place?
ELEANOR: [*softly*] I've had a lifetime to learn forgiveness. For my absent father who left home, for Franklin who has never left his family home, and for friends who speak freely.

SCENE FOUR

WINSTON CHURCHILL'*s letter to Franklin D. Roosevelt.*

CHURCHILL: [*spoken live or recorded*] 'My dear Mr President. To sum up the objectives, winning the war in the West in 1942 […] can only be achieved if British and American naval and air superiority in the Atlantic is maintained […] The heavy losses inflicted by Japan upon the United States and British Forces in the Pacific theatre has given the Japanese, for the time being, superiority in these vast waters.' Regarding our objective to set up the unified American, British, Dutch, and Australian command for the South-West Pacific, 'it seems to me that this can't be held anymore. I suggest this enclosed factual statement should be issued around two p.m., which will give the United States morning and evening papers their run, but let the British morning papers have it also for Sunday morning. I cannot fit in the Australian times as the world will keep turning around. Please let me know yr wishes. Yours ever, Winston S. Churchill.'

SCENE FIVE

ELEANOR *and* MARY ALICE.

MARY ALICE: At least Churchill is visiting you.

ELEANOR: Franklin and Churchill talk naval history into the night. I get upset because Franklin gets tired sitting up in his wheelchair.

MARY ALICE: He enjoys it.

ELEANOR: He drinks too much.

MARY ALICE: He's clever the way he converses without actually revealing his views.

ELEANOR: Even to me. No-one believes me. I suspect not even you or Mr Evatt.

MARY ALICE: Perhaps not.

ELEANOR: You know my visit has put out the American generals completely and especially MacArthur.

MARY ALICE: Surely not in Australia.

ELEANOR: They think I'm spying on them.

    Pause.

MARY ALICE: Do they?

ELEANOR: They think the President listens to what I say far too much.

MARY ALICE: You can reach him in an unofficial way.

ELEANOR: They consider the middle-aged wife a poor substitute for the President. Our brass on Noumea were particularly unhappy. I think the trouble I cause far outweighs the momentary interest it may give the soldiers to see me.

MARY ALICE: They'll talk about your visit for weeks.

ELEANOR: They'd prefer Rita Hayworth.

MARY ALICE: You remind them of their mother.

ELEANOR: I make them homesick. Some even cry.

    Pause.

MARY ALICE: They know your three sons are fighting, like our Peter.

ELEANOR: I take names and addresses to contact the families when I get back.

MARY ALICE: Surely the generals can't complain about that.

ELEANOR: But I need to do more than walk miles in hospital wards.

MARY ALICE: It's exhausting.
ELEANOR: Is that your experience too?
MARY ALICE: I carry reminders of home, Eleanor.
ELEANOR: What do you take?
MARY ALICE: I travel with pictures and … a frame.
ELEANOR: A frame?
MARY ALICE: Some pictures have to have a frame.
ELEANOR: Franklin will be amused. He's keen to hear about Dr Evatt. He listened carefully to the judge's views on British precedent over the American Constitution in '35.
MARY ALICE: Bert is not so ardent about anything British these days. He thinks they've abandoned us.
ELEANOR: Even British law?
MARY ALICE: Lawyers might be good talkers, but Franklin is a good listener, too.
ELEANOR: [*sighing*] What do you want me to tell him, Mary Alice?
MARY ALICE: Tell him about the dinner tonight.
ELEANOR: Is that it?
MARY ALICE: I trust you to report what is said.
ELEANOR: Mr Evatt's persuasive about Churchill's … bias against Australia.
MARY ALICE: I knew you'd understand! They might joke Bert is eating his way to power, but we know who has to do the catering.
ELEANOR: He certainly dominates the table when he starts remembering all those cricket scores back through the years.
MARY ALICE: [*laughing*] Whether it's football or cricket, winning the game is an Australian thing.
ELEANOR: Winning is an American thing.

SCENE SIX

FRANKLIN ROOSEVELT*'s letter to Winston Churchill.*

ROOSEVELT: [*spoken live or recorded*] 'Secret and Personal for the Former Naval Person from the President.' The Australian War Council and the New Zealanders want an equal voice on a Pacific command based in Washington. Herbert Evatt was here for six weeks and very persuasive. The staff's 'general feeling, with which I concur, is that all political and governmental matters concerning New Zealand, Australia and the Netherlands East Indies should continue to be handled in London and the military matters be resolved here' in Washington. The staff 'will invite their participants in discussion of such matters as involve their national interests.'

'August 11, 1943. From President to the Prime Minister. Suggest thin clothes to be prepared for a variety of weather. Delighted to see you in any costume. Roosevelt.'

SCENE SEVEN

ELEANOR *and* MARY ALICE.

MARY ALICE: There has to be more to life than trying to find proper food for the family or material to keep them clothed.
ELEANOR: In my experience, women worry more about where to get furniture for their homes, if they have one, than what to put on the walls.
MARY ALICE: But a painting can make a home anywhere.
ELEANOR: I'm not sure my readers would choose this painting. Years ago, we helped start a furniture factory for unemployed locals.
MARY ALICE: Once I could not imagine living without painting.
ELEANOR: Has the war changed that?
MARY ALICE: It's harder to justify.
ELEANOR: Men cannot live—

MARY ALICE joins in.

ELEANOR and MARY ALICE: [*together*] —by bread alone.

Both women smile at each other.

MARY ALICE: [*shrugging*] In Paris I was still free to study painting for two wonderful months. Studio time is now impossible.
ELEANOR: Solitude is rare.
MARY ALICE: Do you write about that in your column?

Pause.

ELEANOR: No. It would seem like I wanted to do nothing and give my husband's critics some serious ammunition to shoot me down.

Pause.

MARY ALICE: Franklin took such pride in showing me paintings round your home.

ELEANOR: His mother's house. We've never had a home of our own. I have a cabin. I'm away often.

Pause.

MARY ALICE: Spring in Paris seems miraculous to someone from Australia. The horizon of grey roofs pressed low by a muddy sky, suddenly bursting open. Bright green springing out of dry trees; pink blossoms reigning overhead; and daffodils bowing below. It's a painter's dream.

She is moving.

I woke early one morning to see a gigantic full moon hovering just above the rooftops, a luminous white globe, the strangest thing I'd seen. I stood transfixed. It was unbelievably beautiful and ominous at the same time. It made me sad, I didn't know why.

ELEANOR: A premonition?
MARY ALICE: Australia has been cut off.
ELEANOR: Planes are getting through now.
MARY ALICE: They bring official war news.
ELEANOR: [*slowly*] But no news of Moya.
MARY ALICE: I'd like to know she's … well.

Pause.

ELEANOR: I could ask what can be found out.
MARY ALICE: I'd be grateful.

SCENE EIGHT

ELEANOR *and* MARY ALICE.

ELEANOR: Some of my most treasured wedding presents are watercolours … of Venice. How does Moya get time to paint?
MARY ALICE: She's married to Sam Ateyo, he's a painter too. Some women forego family life …
ELEANOR: And public life.
MARY ALICE: Art's very public and—
ELEANOR: Symbolic.
MARY ALICE: —intimate at the same time
ELEANOR: Do you think art can have a supernatural effect?
MARY ALICE: Painting can be mysterious.

ELEANOR: There was a sculpture of Franklin as a young man before he got polio that oddly stops at the knees …
MARY ALICE: I think art should stir us and not merely record the passing of time. It should make us feel part of something bigger.
ELEANOR: I see.
MARY ALICE: It's nearly time we went back.
ELEANOR: Must we? I'm just beginning to enjoy Australia. I need—
MARY ALICE: That's a relief.
ELEANOR: I need your advice. I do everything across a barrier of fear.
MARY ALICE: We have nothing to fear—

> ELEANOR *joins in.*

MARY ALICE and ELEANOR: [*together*] —but fear itself.
ELEANOR: But with enough imagination—
MARY ALICE: I want every Australian to visit a gallery.
ELEANOR: Art was never one of my mother's priorities. In her world you were kind to the poor. You did not neglect your philanthropic duties.
MARY ALICE: Were you close to your father?
ELEANOR: I was his 'Little Nell'.
MARY ALICE: Nell?
ELEANOR: After the Dickens character.
MARY ALICE: I was too rebellious to please my father
ELEANOR: My father sent letters and stories urging me to grow up brave and educated, which is not what my beautiful, disapproving mother expected of me.
MARY ALICE: I learnt how to argue opposing my father.
ELEANOR: I disappointed him when I lacked physical courage.
MARY ALICE: Your father would not be disappointed in you now.
ELEANOR: But he'd expect me to know more about art.
MARY ALICE: I'm here to help.
ELEANOR: My friends have been writers.
MARY ALICE: Not anymore. Art and love both start with a promise …
ELEANOR: Those closest, I love deeply, then for the rest of the world, I fear.
MARY ALICE: Will we ever get through this brutality?
ELEANOR: We must.
MARY ALICE: We fight best when what we love is threatened.

> *Pause.*

ACT ONE

ELEANOR: But can we kill if we don't hate?
MARY ALICE: We must know what we fight for.
ELEANOR: The chance to end war and a lasting peace ... and human rights.
MARY ALICE: Franklin wants freedom of speech and religion and freedom from hunger and fear.

SCENE NINE

WINSTON CHURCHILL*'s letter to Franklin Roosevelt.*

CHURCHILL: [*spoken live or recorded*] 'Hyde Park, New York State. August 13, 1943. My dear Franklin, thinking things over would it not be better to go straight from here to the Citadel & let us [my wife and I] come back here and to the White House after the Conference? The eyes of the World are on the Conference [...] I do not know of course how important or urgent is yr business in Washington, but I am quite sure the sooner we are up North again the better. W.'

SCENE TEN

ELEANOR *and* MARY ALICE.

ELEANOR: I need your advice about Sydney.
MARY ALICE: The harbour is very beautiful.
ELEANOR: I'm to speak at the Town Hall and for the radio.
MARY ALICE: I know.
ELEANOR: I need your guidance—
MARY ALICE: I'm not sure—
ELEANOR: I'm worried about delivering a good performance.
MARY ALICE: The crowd will come to see you.
ELEANOR: That's what worries me. Everyone will be listening carefully.
MARY ALICE: You've done so many public speeches.
ELEANOR: Not in Australia.
MARY ALICE: I'm not sure that I can help.
ELEANOR: You give speeches.
MARY ALICE: Three years ago for Bert's election campaign.
ELEANOR: How should I approach it?
MARY ALICE: These days, I only do the catering for the women's meetings in his electorate. They let me serve coffee instead of tea.

ELEANOR: [*smiling*] And I have to offer tea back home.

Pause.

MARY ALICE: How was it in New Zealand?

ELEANOR: I was more relaxed after I was greeted nose to nose by the wonderful Rangi.

Pause.

Today I stood at the official reception expecting the Aboriginal leader to arrive.

MARY ALICE: You'll be waiting a long time in Canberra.

ELEANOR: Rangi christened me Kotoku, which means white heron in Maori. Should I recount that story in Sydney?

MARY ALICE: [*hesitantly*] The crowd will be full of workers.

ELEANOR: They can be the toughest audience, especially if they've been out of work.

MARY ALICE: Lots of women workers these days.

ELEANOR: Then I should speak about how women's labour will help us win this war.

MARY ALICE: [*laughing*] That crowd will listen to that message.

ELEANOR: But will they be persuaded by me? Sometimes it's hard to see the gains.

MARY ALICE: From public speaking?

ELEANOR: Public speaking by the wife.

MARY ALICE: People are curious. That's an advantage.

ELEANOR: I—I'm criticised whatever I say.

MARY ALICE: I've been advised not to sound too authoritative.

ELEANOR: Otherwise everyone thinks *you're* in power.

MARY ALICE: And not to sound like a know-all and not to speak about—

ELEANOR *joins in.*

MARY ALICE and ELEANOR: [*together*] —politics.

ELEANOR: Only talk about cooking and fashion! But surely you're allowed to speak about art?

MARY ALICE: Not really, even though I'm to be a trustee of the New South Wales Art Gallery.

ELEANOR: You can really do some good.

MARY ALICE: [*quietly*] I hope so.

ACT ONE   13

ELEANOR: Do you have doubts?

> MARY ALICE *nods.*

You know so much about modern art.

MARY ALICE: The authorities don't like that I'm a woman and that I'm Bert's wife.

ELEANOR: He's adamant that you are the better speaker and he's unstoppable.

MARY ALICE: But it's a struggle to convince people that art is important even during peacetime.

ELEANOR: I suspect that you are very persuasive.

MARY ALICE: And I can't think of a more sincere speaker for the war effort. But you had better not tell anyone else that you have been dreading your visit to Australia.

ELEANOR: Perhaps you should only discuss how paintings *swing* in private.

SCENE ELEVEN

FRANKLIN ROOSEVELT*'s letter.*

ROOSEVELT: [*spoken live or recorded*] 'August 28, 1943. Two forty-five p.m.. From the President to Colonel Warden. Personal and Secret. It is a coincidence that I was on the point of sending you a suggestion for an interim message to Uncle Joe when yours came this morning. Therefore, I am sending the one you suggest via the Russian Embassy in Washington. I am delighted as Quebec papers say, you are teasing the trout, but I did not believe New York newspaper accounts that you have landed a five-pounder fishing. I shall require sworn verification. We are looking forward to your arrival Wednesday evening. We will be listening to you on the air on Tuesday.'

SCENE TWELVE

ELEANOR *and* MARY ALICE.

MARY ALICE: I thought Franklin was joking at that party he gave us in Washington last year, saying he guessed his missus might visit us.

ELEANOR: A diversion. I was invited to visit China and Russia and he was against it.

MARY ALICE: Wouldn't the plane flight have been much, much safer?

ELEANOR: Greater political risks.

MARY ALICE: We were surprised you were allowed to fly to Australia. There are countless dangers during the flight.

ELEANOR: But I need to really show the soldiers that I'm not afraid.

MARY ALICE: Were you briefed on using the lifeboat raft? [*Imitating a male naval pilot*] 'Well now, if by any chance the plane should be shot down and we had to leave the plane … Now what you must do, you must blow up the raft, but don't start to blow until you've jumped out of the plane, do it in mid-air. Then climb on to the raft and you'll find a fishing line and a knife concealed in a portion of the raft. Start fishing immediately …' [*laughing*] or starve.

ELEANOR: [*laughing*] I can't swim and I don't like boats.

MARY ALICE: I'm not sure I can eat raw fish.

ELEANOR: Let's hope we don't have to put that to the test.

MARY ALICE: We could have made it as far as Russia last year. After we visited you and Franklin, we had to wait for a strong tailwind to blow us across the Atlantic to England. We had a very, very good Canadian pilot determined to save petrol and break the time record and he flew us high up in the heart of the wind. [*Dryly*] He was enjoying himself and sent back a note: 'We've sighted the coast of England. Shall I keep going? There's enough petrol to get to Moscow.'

ELEANOR: [*laughing*] What's a flight over enemy lines after you've flown all the way across the Pacific from Australia?

MARY ALICE: The officials in England were very, very put out because we were two hours early.

ELEANOR: You're not forgiven when you upset their schedule. Last year, on my trip to England, I learnt how to get unscheduled meetings into the day with our soldiers and the women in factories. I took my secretary, Tommy, to England and she helped.

MARY ALICE: She might have helped this trip?

ELEANOR: I decided to come alone.

MARY ALICE: Because of the danger?

Pause.

ELEANOR: Tommy's not an early riser.

Pause.

MARY ALICE: I find it very hard to leave our Rosalind behind. But I have no choice. Bert's Minister for External Affairs and he has to go. He's convinced we'll need an aviation industry after the war. But he won't fly anywhere without me.
ELEANOR: I must show the soldiers.

SCENE THIRTEEN

WINSTON CHURCHILL's *letters to Franklin Roosevelt.*

CHURCHILL: [*spoken live or recorded*] 'August 30, 1943. From Colonel Warden to the President. My wife Clemmie has benefited from her rest up here and would very much like to come back with us to Washington if you still have room. She would not be able to undertake any public engagements.'

'Mr President. It seemed to me that your draft message to Stalin did not draw a clear enough distinction between the Mediterranean Commission and the Three-Power Conference. I have ventured therefore to suggest some alterations […] I also annex a re-draft of my message.'

SCENE FOURTEEN

ELEANOR *and* MARY ALICE.

ELEANOR: I got up early to join the rank and file for breakfast at Honolulu, on Wallis, Christmas, Bora Bora. Even Samoa.

Pause.

Our young soldiers asked me if they will have work after the war.
MARY ALICE: They *must* dream about the future, otherwise … Up in the air, you see differently. Last year, when we flew out of Hawaii, imagine, there was a sunset lasting two hours. Did you find Palmyra the most beautiful of the islands?
ELEANOR: I might have enjoyed seeing it under different circumstances.
MARY ALICE: We need to see that beauty so we don't get despondent. My first wartime flight was such a shock. Bert and I had to write notes

to each other and his two colleagues. I wore three woollen jumpers, a coat and two headscarves. You get used to the noise and lack of pressure, but not the cold, the below zero cold.

ELEANOR: I still don't think the flight here is enough.

MARY ALICE: What else can you do?

ELEANOR: I've discovered that malaria is as bad as bullets on those islands. The soldiers' hardship is overwhelming.

MARY ALICE: And food rots very quickly.

ELEANOR: I've heard. There's a big difference between officers' lives and the men's, and nothing provided for the black soldiers.

MARY ALICE: And no-one reports back. I had to tell your Minister of Supply that the soldiers on Canton Island needed cement mixers and bulldozers to make bomb shelters. It's seven miles long, with only one tree, and the Japanese planes bomb it regularly.

ELEANOR: I try to keep my personal views to myself because of Franklin's position. I asked him not to tell me anything of great importance so I would not let something slip and cause trouble. He relies on me. On what I see. I'm his legs, so to speak.

MARY ALICE: And his eyes.

ELEANOR: He does trust me.

MARY ALICE: So do the servicemen.

ELEANOR: That's why I have to make this trip matter.

MARY ALICE: Believe me, you have.

ELEANOR: I saw Kokoda in that film Mr Evatt brought over last year.

MARY ALICE: It's a frontline!

ELEANOR: Yes.

MARY ALICE: You won't be allowed there.

ELEANOR: I need to face the same risks as the soldiers.

SCENE FIFTEEN

FRANKLIN ROOSEVELT's *letter to Winston Churchill.*

ROOSEVELT: [*spoken live or recorded*] 'From the President to the Former Naval Person. The newspapers here had a field day over General Marshall's duties. The drums were beaten rather loudly by the rest of the press for a few days but it is pretty much of a dead cat now. It seems to me that if we are forced into making public statements about our military commands we will find ourselves with the newspapers running the war. I, therefore, hope that nothing will be said about the business until it is actually accomplished […] I agree with you that we should not permit any undue optimism about this campaign either at home or abroad. The answer that we got from Uncle Joe relative to the Moscow meeting was not unexpected so it seems there is nothing to do but take the trip there and we are organizing accordingly. Roosevelt.'

SCENE SIXTEEN

ELEANOR *and* MARY ALICE.

ELEANOR: Our military leaders are hostile to my plan, Mary Alice. The brass won't let me fly on.
MARY ALICE: I'm not surprised.
ELEANOR: I fly all this way only to be stopped.
MARY ALICE: You and I had to get an exemption to fly at all.
ELEANOR: Surely you're not agreeing with them?
MARY ALICE: You can't go further.
ELEANOR: My visit must matter.
MARY ALICE: It's not necessary to go any further.
ELEANOR: Going on would make this whole trip worthwhile.
MARY ALICE: You'll feel differently after you've given your speech in Sydney.
ELEANOR: It's not enough. This trip will only be worthwhile if I visit Guadalcanal.
MARY ALICE: But there's fighting on the Solomon Islands.
ELEANOR: Yes.
MARY ALICE: What if something happens to you?
ELEANOR: I need to show the soldiers.
MARY ALICE: Not even our leaders are expected to visit. It's the battlefront! The military are afraid the American President's wife might become a casualty of war on their patch. They don't want the responsibility.
ELEANOR: You said yourself something could happen on any part of the flight back home. You're just trying to talk me out of going near the fighting.
MARY ALICE: Everyone else is being polite about the risks.

ELEANOR: Military leaders visit the battlefront.
MARY ALICE: But not their wives.
ELEANOR: The President is Commander.
MARY ALICE: The Commander's wife doesn't go to a battlefront.
ELEANOR: Because she's the wife?
MARY ALICE: A civilian.
ELEANOR: A woman civilian?
MARY ALICE: I mean everyone sent there is military.
ELEANOR: Franklin would visit the battlefront if he could.
MARY ALICE: Would he?
ELEANOR: But he can't go. Franklin needs someone to lean on just to stand up.
MARY ALICE: Has anyone asked Franklin about your plan?
ELEANOR: Not expressly.
MARY ALICE: He'd say no.
ELEANOR: I have a friend stationed there. Joe is there.
MARY ALICE: Ahh. You know you will get a genuine welcome.
ELEANOR: You've been asked to talk me out of trying to go.

Pause.

MARY ALICE: Not exactly.
ELEANOR: To distract me?
MARY ALICE: To suggest alternatives.
ELEANOR: You can't.
MARY ALICE: What can I do to make you forget this crazy idea?

Pause.

ELEANOR: My extended trip could improve Australian-American relations.
MARY ALICE: I have no influence.
ELEANOR: Mr Evatt does.
MARY ALICE: Not over the American Army.
ELEANOR: I need your support. I need to go.
MARY ALICE: You know we lost an engine on our second return trip across the Pacific.
ELEANOR: You made it back. It's extraordinary what those pilots do. Someone hung a lump of lead on a string out of the plane to measure the wind speed. Chewing gum and string. How those boys make do is the war's best-kept secret.

MARY ALICE: You are the *only one* who thinks you should go.
ELEANOR: They're naming the plane 'Our Eleanor'. I'm not sure if I am flattered. But I intend to make full use of my namesake.

    Pause.

MARY ALICE: You're determined.
ELEANOR: I am.
MARY ALICE: It's reckless.
ELEANOR: Can you talk to your husband …
MARY ALICE: I have no idea what Bert will say.
ELEANOR: But you'll talk to him?
MARY ALICE: Against my better judgment, for you.

    They exit together arm in arm.

END OF ACT ONE

ACT TWO

SCENE SEVENTEEN

ELEANOR *and* MARY ALICE.

Paris, 1948.

MARY ALICE *and* ELEANOR *greet each other warmly.*

MARY ALICE: *Bonjour, Eleanor, bonjour.*
ELEANOR: *Bonjour, ma chère amie.* Good to see you again, Mary Alice.
MARY ALICE: And you, Eleanor.

    Pause.

ELEANOR: I'm pleased you wanted to meet.
MARY ALICE: I'm grateful you could find time with all your new responsibilities.
ELEANOR: I'm sorry it'll be short.
MARY ALICE: Please don't apologise.
ELEANOR: I saw you observing the UN General Assembly.
MARY ALICE: I've a card of entry because of Bert's position. How did you get away?
ELEANOR: I was determined …
MARY ALICE: [*smiling*] Like you were determined to get to the battlefront?
ELEANOR: I flew there in the dark. I was right. It did matter to the soldiers.
MARY ALICE: I bet those GIs were very surprised to have the President's wife drop by.
ELEANOR: You tried hard to persuade me …
MARY ALICE: About modern art! Did you see your friend?
ELEANOR: We had one hour in a dark night.

    Pause.

  How is your artist friend?
MARY ALICE: Moya's back here in Paris, thank you.
ELEANOR: Are you enjoying Paris?
MARY ALICE: Very, very much. I love Paris even with this chill in the air. The late autumn light hides the pitted stone.

ELEANOR: It's restful here outside the Palais.
MARY ALICE: This outlook down to the Eiffel Tower makes it almost golden.
ELEANOR: The fountain is calming. I need an excuse to leave the battles inside.
MARY ALICE: I'll give you an excuse anytime.
ELEANOR: And I thought you wouldn't want to meet me.
MARY ALICE: But why would I avoid you?
ELEANOR: Mr Evatt would expect your support.
MARY ALICE: Try keeping me away!
ELEANOR: You're not upset with me?
MARY ALICE: You're my friend.
ELEANOR: I was anxious.
MARY ALICE: Because of Bert?
ELEANOR: He had every right to be upset.
MARY ALICE: Loyalty is not the same thing as agreeing with everything Bert does or says. You know that.
ELEANOR: It's a relief to hear you say it. Does Bert know my committee is still arguing over the wording, especially the Russians and delegates from Muslim countries.
MARY ALICE: I know he wants to get the General Assembly behind human rights and the Declaration.

SCENE EIGHTEEN

HERBERT EVATT'*s lecture.*

EVATT: [*spoken live or recorded, as if giving a speech*] Fortunately, the peace settlement with Japan poses far fewer difficulties than those which delayed the European settlements. The Far Eastern Commission established at Washington to lay down the general principles of Allied occupation policy in Japan consists of the eleven countries which took an active part in the war in the Pacific [...] Decisions should require only a two-thirds majority. This would eliminate any Great Power veto [...] I must emphasise again that the United Nations Organisation was never intended to frame the peace settlements [...] The case for considering Korea is far stronger, as a deadlock on this subject has developed outside the United Nations between the Soviet Union and the United States.

SCENE NINETEEN

ELEANOR *and* MARY ALICE.

ELEANOR: Shall we sit for a moment?
MARY ALICE: You look tired.
ELEANOR: My feet ache. Standing at receptions over the years has damaged a bone in my instep.
MARY ALICE: I need advice about a reception. I'm dreading it.
ELEANOR: Which one?
MARY ALICE: The garden party in the Parc de Bagatelle with the King and Queen. I don't want to make any mistakes.
ELEANOR: I know exactly how you feel.
MARY ALICE: The protocol is daunting. Bert is very comfortable conversing at length with the King who likes to hear what he has to say. That puts me in the limelight for much too long.
ELEANOR: I understand. The thought of three days at Buckingham Palace terrified me more than that flight to Australia.
MARY ALICE: Thankfully we've never been invited to stay at Buckingham Palace.
ELEANOR: No-one criticises the Queen for her meals.
MARY ALICE: What's your advice?
ELEANOR: Be yourself. Discuss the garden.

Pause.

The Bagatelle château has a formal garden and a rose garden.
MARY ALICE: I should recognise roses and I can talk about our garden of Australian natives.
ELEANOR: [*giggling*] Take care not to trip over those little hedges when all eyes are on you.
MARY ALICE: It could be far worse.
ELEANOR: You could have to do the catering.

    MARY ALICE *laughs.*

MARY ALICE: I can talk about wandering around Paris.
ELEANOR: I'd advise you to talk about gardens and parks. I am pleased the United Nations General Assembly has elected your Bert as its President.

MARY ALICE: And we're very happy that you are chairing the UN Human Rights Committee.

ELEANOR: Is *he*?

MARY ALICE: [*smiling*] Bert is delighted the American delegation thought they had neatly sidelined you to the least important committee.

ELEANOR: I was willing.

MARY ALICE: It's becoming the most important committee because of the refugees.

ELEANOR: Everyone thought I would be out of the way, including me.

MARY ALICE: Only people who don't know you would believe that.

Pause.

ELEANOR: It should be Franklin.

MARY ALICE: You were always a team.

ELEANOR: I never wanted to be a president's wife. I do *not* miss co-ordinating the White House dinners for one minute. I could not please anyone. I was criticised as 'mean' if I served basic fare and criticised as 'wasteful' if I served more elaborate cuisine.

MARY ALICE: The food was always incidental to the conversation.

ELEANOR: Only to you.

MARY ALICE: You and Franklin made everyone welcome.

ELEANOR: He liked people.

MARY ALICE: You must miss him terribly. The news was a great, great shock to all his friends.

ELEANOR: It wasn't until he died that I realised how much I relied on our conversations.

MARY ALICE: His death coming so close to the end of the war was like another casualty.

Pause.

I can't imagine life without Bert.

ELEANOR: To the world, Franklin was always cheerful. He kept his pain to himself all those years. He could barely stay on his feet for thirty minutes.

MARY ALICE: He leaned on you.

ELEANOR: Actually, our son helped him stand. But I was accustomed to doing things … around his work needs.

MARY ALICE: We do that for people we love.

ELEANOR: We do. What does Mr Evatt expect of you?

MARY ALICE: I need to stay cheerful.
ELEANOR: Your smile will win over everyone.

SCENE TWENTY

HERBERT EVATT's *lecture*.

EVATT: [*spoken live or recorded*] Irresponsible use of the veto in the Security Council has done great harm to the prestige of the United Nations and the Assembly […] Two of the permanent members of the Council, the United States and China, have now publicly adhered to the view that the veto upon Pacific settlement of disputes should not be exercised in practice although they have not proposed amending the Charter. Australia, supported by many other countries, fought at San Francisco to limit the veto to enforcement action only.

SCENE TWENTY-ONE

ELEANOR *and* MARY ALICE.

MARY ALICE: Rosalind and I saw a Punch and Judy show in the Parc Monceau this morning.
ELEANOR: The old Paris returns to life.
MARY ALICE: It's sad and wounded.
ELEANOR: But here for my grandchildren to visit one day.
MARY ALICE: How many now?
ELEANOR: Thirteen. I start Christmas shopping in January.
MARY ALICE: No wonder you look tired.

Pause.

Look at that bird hopping about with grass pieces hanging out of its beak. All that effort for such a fragile nest.

Pause.

I remember when Bert and I first arrived for the Peace Conference two years ago in '46. Paris was quiet, emptied of vehicles, and the only fighting was in the north. The air was lilac scented. There were weddings, like the birth of a new innocence. The wedding party arrived on bicycles. The United Nations was scarcely a paper dream.

We were so busy then just getting basic supplies. Moya got firewood and blankets for the Australians.

Pause.

I walked through a park with plane trees and cypresses. There were old people sitting on benches turned to the sun like pale daffodil faces. It was like nothing had happened and yet the world had changed completely.

Pause.

There was such a feeling of hostility among the delegates.

ELEANOR: Some delegates still have no freedom to decide anything.

MARY ALICE: They can decide which paintings to take home. The great paintings are coming back. I was wrong that art is outside war.

ELEANOR: I was wrong about a war to end all wars.

MARY ALICE: I want to believe in something bigger. The work that you and Bert are doing is very, very important. Come to the Parc Monceau, Rosalind and I usually say goodbye to Bert outside a café that's eighty years old and amble down the Rue de Rembrandt.

ELEANOR: I could meet Mr Evatt there one morning for breakfast.

MARY ALICE: He's at work early.

ELEANOR: Mr Evatt has no time to sit in a café?

MARY ALICE: Not these days. But please come with Rosalind and I. It's like stepping back in time with stone ruins from bygone empires, in among the trees and old cast-iron lampposts.

ELEANOR: It sounds untouched.

MARY ALICE: The Parc Monceau has reminders. In the little museum I saw some old oriental sculptures, such beautiful very, very early carvings. But a fearful beauty. They were used to hide Resistance weapons.

ELEANOR: Reminders of the war are everywhere.

SCENE TWENTY-TWO

HERBERT EVATT's *papers.*

EVATT: [*spoken live or recorded, reading from a report*] 'We would like to require members to pledge themselves to take action both national and international for the purpose of securing for all peoples, including their own, improved labour standards, economic advancement, employment for all, and social security.'

'The Declaration of Human Rights will have great moral force as a standard, and helps to explain the general references to human rights contained in the United Nations Charter […] Australia has from the beginning been one of the leaders in this field.'

SCENE TWENTY-THREE

ELEANOR *and* MARY ALICE.

MARY ALICE: Moya thinks Picasso is the greatest and Picasso thinks Matisse is the greatest artist.
ELEANOR: You've met Picasso?
MARY ALICE: I visit his studio where the Resistance used to meet. Bert is put out that he can't come.

   Pause.

ELEANOR: Is he?

   Pause.

MARY ALICE: You think Bert is easily put out. Picasso has a broken heart about the military conservatism in Spain and yearns for a much more modern way, but not the Soviet communist one. We're trying to get Picasso to come to the Assembly. He hesitates because he's worried there will be demonstrations against him.
ELEANOR: What if the three of us visited Picasso together?
MARY ALICE: I'm not sure Bert has the time to go.
ELEANOR: It's probably not a task for a president.
MARY ALICE: If he did go, Picasso could hardly refuse the two of you?
ELEANOR: Do you really think he can help?
MARY ALICE: He's passionate.
ELEANOR: That matters.

   Pause.

MARY ALICE: I'm trying to decide what art to take back to Australia. I've seen some wonderful works by Modigliani.
ELEANOR: Would I like them?
MARY ALICE: Let me show you.
ELEANOR: I visited Peggy Guggenheim's gallery in New York four years ago, after Australia, but found the art …

MARY ALICE: Mysterious?

ELEANOR: I liked meeting her artist friends.

MARY ALICE I suspect that you value art in the abstract but not abstract art.

ELEANOR: But I really admire some artists, Mary Alice.

MARY ALICE: Come to lunch with us.

ELEANOR: I'd really like that. I could consult Bert.

MARY ALICE: Bert rarely joins us for lunch anymore.

They begin walking.

The other day we stood watching two ducks paddling with great difficulty near the waterline for a long time. Then suddenly they just flew away, and so effortlessly.

ELEANOR: So Mr Evatt had time to watch ducks?

MARY ALICE: Rosalind and I. And Moya.

ELEANOR: Your husband, Mr Evatt, our champion of small nations, is upset with me.

MARY ALICE: He hates wasting time.

ELEANOR: I'm sorry it happened.

MARY ALICE: It's not your fault he was kept waiting.

ELEANOR: I won't make him wait again.

MARY ALICE: He feels that he can't waste a moment.

ELEANOR: What can I do to help?

MARY ALICE: [*sighing*] What hope has anyone of working together if even you and Bert are at odds?

SCENE TWENTY-FOUR

HERBERT EVATT's *papers.*

EVATT: [*spoken live or recorded, talking in a conversational way*] 'Not much traffic today, Bundy. A fast drive. That's good. Do you think it helps that I don't fit the image of a president? It falls on my shoulders to make the General Assembly run smoothly. The President should also provide leadership on policy and find a way of making fifty-eight nations reach some agreement. It's a herculean task. It's good that smaller nations see us Australians as not aligned with the big nations. After you dropped me off yesterday for the opening of the General Assembly, that gendarme on the steps stopped me from entering the building. He thought I looked like a troublemaker and should be barred from attending. You'd better wait a little today to make sure they let me inside.'

SCENE TWENTY-FIVE

ELEANOR *and* MARY ALICE.

MARY ALICE: Bert thinks everyone in the world should be a citizen of the UN, not just the stateless refugees.
ELEANOR: Getting everyone to agree on that one might be hard.
MARY ALICE: He wants the world to compete through sport, preferably cricket.
ELEANOR: I can't really see the US delegates agreeing to cricket as the international game *par excellence.*
    I have a group of religious friends who claim that the answer to all our difficulties is a great religious revival. They may be right, but short emotional upheavals lifting people to the heights before dropping them down again is not what is needed.
MARY ALICE: But art will not save us.
ELEANOR: No.
MARY ALICE: Instead, it had to be rescued.
ELEANOR: But it mattered.
MARY ALICE: To the few who love it.
ELEANOR: We need a fundamental change in human nature.
MARY ALICE: We can't love the enemy.
ELEANOR: They meet together here, that's a start. Even if my committee can't agree.
MARY ALICE: People can't forget.

    Pause.

Today I saw a plaque for those shot. Taken out and shot in forests for being loyal to their city, their country, their own people. They were patriots.
    You can make peace, but how do you make it durable? How do we overcome bitterness, sadness, desolation?
ELEANOR: Or even rivalry between patriots?
MARY ALICE: That, too.

ELEANOR: I tried to apologise.
MARY ALICE: It's a misunderstanding.
ELEANOR: Outside my control.
MARY ALICE: Yes, I know.
ELEANOR: Does Mr Evatt …?
MARY ALICE: Bert thought he was taking a break from the wrangling over rank.
ELEANOR: They should not have held up proceedings until I arrived.
MARY ALICE: It's not your fault that the French think an American ex-president's widow outranks my husband.
ELEANOR: Only in the provinces.
MARY ALICE: I'm sure the town officials did not know what to do.
ELEANOR: Your husband was their guest of honour.
MARY ALICE: And so he was.
ELEANOR: But they kept him waiting for me.
MARY ALICE: It's not personal. He's concerned that the French slighted Australia when the officials waited for you to arrive. He thinks he *is* Australia over here.
ELEANOR: Helped by the press.
MARY ALICE: He's under pressure.
ELEANOR: We can't be just Eleanor and Bert to the outside world. Bert's French is improving. That speech was very good. His annoyance with me did not show.
MARY ALICE: You hold the same ideals.
ELEANOR: I admire the way Mr Evatt uses the role of president to push his campaign for full employment. His best tactic was to ask for anyone in the Assembly supporting *un*employment to stand up.

    MARY ALICE *laughs*.

MARY ALICE: Bert works long hours. It makes him short-tempered.
ELEANOR: He's got an impossible job.
MARY ALICE: Maybe more women delegates instead of women translators would improve things.
ELEANOR: We can only hope.
MARY ALICE: Many of the Latin American delegates are women.
ELEANOR: Countries send philosophers as if we are a debating society.
MARY ALICE: [*surprised*] You think there's too much talking?

ELEANOR: Yes. And the press make trouble about the smallest thing.

MARY ALICE: But if you have only one point of view presented all the time it's very bad for people's minds, and it's very bad for their bodies, too.

ELEANOR: We need Hick, we kneed more women reporters.

MARY ALICE: Like the one who did all the UN profiles in San Francisco?

ELEANOR: Caroline Anspacker. Your husband seemed to be her favourite.

MARY ALICE: I know! I was there.

ELEANOR: [*smiling*] Welcome to the club. You don't have to worry. I had to accept that my marriage was crowded.

MARY ALICE: It's very hard to accept that even my middle-aged Bert, in spectacles with his tie all askew and his crumpled suit, attracts … female attention.

ELEANOR: The attractions of strong personality and … power.

MARY ALICE: We need more women delegates, like Jessie Street, who understand power.

SCENE TWENTY-SIX

HERBERT EVATT*'s papers.*

EVATT: [*spoken live or recorded*] 'Some think I can snap my fingers and make everyone agree. Sam, I have come to realise that there is no other way to this one. I hate to admit this, but the only way out is partition. There's no compromise to be found because the two sides are so far apart. Palestine will have to be divided. [*Pausing*] Call Bundy and tell him I'm ready to drive back to the apartment to have dinner with Mary Alice and Rosalind. Can you apologise to Bundy again, and tell him I will have to come back after dinner to work. I'm sorry but it will be another late night, two in the morning again for us. I'll need to be back at nine tomorrow.'

SCENE TWENTY-SEVEN

ELEANOR *and* MARY ALICE.

MARY ALICE: I can't explain why, but you seem different.

ELEANOR: I have to be forceful to chair the committee. It's against my nature.

ACT TWO 31

MARY ALICE: I thought it might be losing Franklin.

ELEANOR: I was lonely before he died. I'd given up my second chance … I agreed to stay in the marriage. I made the best of everything. Then he became Governor of New York and then President. I'm sad that he did not live to see this UN begin.

MARY ALICE: Would he have been prepared for this long, slow process?

ELEANOR: I don't know.

Pause.

I should not have been appointed to the UN.

MARY ALICE: But you've been able to draw attention to refugees.

ELEANOR: I came full of hope.

MARY ALICE: We came out of the war believing we could keep working together.

ELEANOR: Yet it's as if my erratic social causes have all finally come together at this time in life.

MARY ALICE: I don't envy your task.

ELEANOR: My committee needs more plain-speaking delegates to solve the problems of refugees.

MARY ALICE: What makes people care enough?

ELEANOR: Children. Your Bert is clear that the Children's Emergency Fund has stirred Australians to support the United Nations refugees.

MARY ALICE: Australia supports renewal of the Fund.

ELEANOR: The Americans are proposing not to renew. Young people are our promise.

MARY ALICE: Providing they get an education.

ELEANOR: We could use the money spent on the military.

MARY ALICE: Would anyone support it? The Russians even vetoed the Red Cross giving a quart of milk per child.

ELEANOR: I like this play about Jefferson where he says, 'We must make war on ignorance and poverty'.

MARY ALICE: We are just beginning to appreciate there's another kind of warfare that you can wage—a warfare through people's hearts and minds.

ELEANOR: We need a science of human relationships.

MARY ALICE: You mean of love and hate?

ELEANOR: Yes, and to stop the suffering. I cannot take it in. In the Jewish refugee camps, every face I saw seemed to represent a story more tragic

than the last. The British are keeping them in camps. All displaced people must be given freedom of choice. I fear our Congress will not listen and not let them into the US.
MARY ALICE: And our government will follow yours.
ELEANOR: That's what I fear.
MARY ALICE: Bert tries.
ELEANOR: The General Assembly listen to him.
MARY ALICE: He believes that people must learn to live with opposing views.
ELEANOR: Does he indeed?!
MARY ALICE: He does. He presided over the committee debating the Jewish and Arab state.
ELEANOR: I know.
MARY ALICE: But how do we break down the barriers?
ELEANOR: I invite my committee to tea to try and smooth over their quibbling about whether we are 'human beings' or 'men and women', or whether we can be free as well as equal, or whether human rights start at birth or conception.
MARY ALICE: Where do you get the energy to keep going?
ELEANOR: You think I should keep my pledge to put on my little lace cap and sit by the fire.
MARY ALICE: I can't really see you as Whistler's mother.
ELEANOR: I'm accepting a doctorate in Civil Law from Oxford University in November, on behalf of American women …
MARY ALICE: That is very, very good news for all women. Dr Roosevelt should be a match for Dr Evatt.
ELEANOR: Not on cricket scores.
MARY ALICE: I heard that some are lobbying to make you the US Secretary of State.
ELEANOR: Please do not wish anything like that appointment on me.
MARY ALICE: Imagine the number of letters.
ELEANOR: [*laughing*] These days I'm an ordinary citizen.
MARY ALICE: Not to the French.
ELEANOR: Or to Bert.
MARY ALICE: He likes to ride the Metro.
ELEANOR: I bet the security guards are not happy about that.
MARY ALICE: They have to chase him in their little motor cars. I go along to watch the fun.

ACT TWO 33

ELEANOR: I'm coming, too.
MARY ALICE: I suspect everyone will try and stop you.
ELEANOR: I'm coming as a protest. My Muslim chauffeur is being dismissed on an exaggerated charge of forging petrol coupons during the war. But I hear it's because his mother's restaurant is a meeting place for Moroccan nationalists against France. Which Metro station?

SCENE TWENTY-EIGHT

HERBERT EVATT'*s papers.*

EVATT: [*spoken live or recorded, delivering a talk*] 'It is the first occasion on which the organised community of nations has made a Declaration of Human Rights and Fundamental Freedoms. That document is backed by the authority of the body of opinion of the United Nations as a whole and millions of people—men, women, and children, all over the world—would turn to it for help, guidance and inspiration.' 'All human beings are born free and equal in dignity and rights ... Everyone is entitled to all the rights and freedoms ...'

SCENE TWENTY-NINE

ELEANOR *and* MARY ALICE.

ELEANOR: I plan to dine at the Moroccan restaurant.
MARY ALICE: We could meet there.
ELEANOR: You could invite Bert and Moya ...
MARY ALICE: It's awkward.
ELEANOR: He has to eat dinner.
MARY ALICE: For Moya. Sam Ateyo works for Bert as his secretary. Moya and Sam were married until recently.
ELEANOR: Then invite Picasso instead.
MARY ALICE: Would he come? He eats at the same restaurant every day.
ELEANOR: The food there must be good.
MARY ALICE: Do you really want to meet Bert at this Moroccan restaurant?
ELEANOR: Meeting there might help.
MARY ALICE: He'll be persuaded by dinner.
ELEANOR: At last!

MARY ALICE: There are so many countries struggling for their independence. We think Asia will become important to Australia.

ELEANOR: Doesn't Bert want to know about the Committee?

MARY ALICE: When will you get your Universal Declaration of Human Rights to the General Assembly?

ELEANOR: [*sighing*] I have to get it by the Russians on my committee. They think it belongs in the eighteenth century.

MARY ALICE: They can only be stopped with a kiss according to one of those Latin-American women.

ELEANOR: Australian jokes resemble Russian ones.

MARY ALICE: I wish they did. For some unknown reason to do with protocol, I am always put next to their Mr Gromyko at official dinners and it is so difficult. I finally found he got excited about concrete and dams. I can talk about water conservation because Bert's brother works with irrigation. Australia never has enough water and there's the problem with salts killing everything except asparagus. Then we found out too much asparagus is not good for the body.

ELEANOR: Too much of anything is bad for us, even idealism.

MARY ALICE: Surely we can't have too much freedom in this Declaration!

ELEANOR: The Committee's four delegates from Muslim countries are concerned over the article giving religious freedom.

MARY ALICE: I suspect they are all questioning the article on the right to the arts. What shall I tell Bert?

ELEANOR: Ask him, can members abstain?

MARY ALICE: That's hopeful.

ELEANOR: You should be a diplomat, Mary Alice.

MARY ALICE: I'd reveal too much.

ELEANOR: You see what has to happen.

MARY ALICE: You're one of the few people I know who could get all those delegates to agree.

ELEANOR: I shut the door. I won't let them leave our evening meeting until they agree. And Bert?

MARY ALICE: Don't worry. He'll agree.

ELEANOR: I see now why you don't get to paint.

MARY ALICE: I would need to shut out the world.

Pause.

ACT TWO

ELEANOR: It appears that the last person to talk to Franklin was his portrait painter.
MARY ALICE: I'm very sorry …
ELEANOR: An artist studies another intimately.
MARY ALICE: So does a committee chair.
ELEANOR: I must go back to the committee. It will be another long night.
MARY ALICE: Good luck.
ELEANOR: It looks like the UN might meet in New York. I will look forward to seeing you there.
MARY ALICE: We'll look at an exhibition together.
ELEANOR: You can explain it to me.
MARY ALICE: That will be a glorious freedom!

They embrace.

ELEANOR: *Au revoir, Mary Alice.*
MARY ALICE: *Au revoir, Eleanor.*

They exit.

THE END

RESEARCH AND QUOTES FROM THE FOLLOWING SOURCES:

Black, Allida M. (ed). (1999) *Courage in a Dangerous World: The Political Writings of Eleanor Roosevelt*, Columbia University Press, 47, 50, 100, 136, 162.

Buckley, Ken, Dale, Barbara, Reynolds, Wayne. (1994) *Doc Evatt*, Melbourne: Longman Cheshire, 312.

Evatt, Herbert Vere. (1948) *The United Nations*, Melbourne: OUP, 53, 102–5, 108.

Hareven, Tamara K. (1968) *Eleanor Roosevelt*, Chicago: Quadrangle Books, 222, 247, 254.

Hogan, Ashley. (2008) *Moving in the Open Daylight: Doc Evatt, an Australian at the United Nations*, Sydney: Sydney University Press, 14, 44, 45.

Kimball, Warren F. (1984) *Churchill & Roosevelt: The Complete Correspondence,* Princeton: Princeton University Press, Vol. I, 298, 312, and Vol. II, 336–7, 382, 386, 388, 434, 437, 439, 489, 491.

Kingsley, Sidney. (1995) 'The Patriots', in *Sidney Kingsley: Five Prizewinning Plays*, edited by Nena Couch, Columbus, Ohio: Ohio State University Press, 223.

Lash, Joseph P. (1971) *Eleanor and Franklin: The Story of their Relationship*, based on Eleanor Roosevelt's private papers. New York: W.W. Norton, 686.

Lash, Joseph P. (1984) *A World of Love*, New York: Doubleday & Company, Inc., 60, 61, 66, 68.

Roosevelt, Eleanor. (1984) *The Autobiography of Eleanor Roosevelt*, Boston: G. K. Hall & Co., 4, 12, 31, 58.

Roosevelt, Eleanor. (1953) *India and the Awakening East,* New York: Harper & Brothers, Publishers, xi, 34, 42.

Roosevelt, Eleanor. (1949) *This I Remember*, New York: Harper & Row, 11, 12.

Rowley, Hazel. (2010) *Franklin and Eleanor*, Melbourne: Melbourne University Press, 67.

Tennant, Kyle. (1970) *Evatt: Politics and Justice*, Sydney: Angus and Robertson, additional information about Mary Alice.

EVATT FOUNDATION AND TASHMADADA

present

Eleanor and Mary Alice

5-8 DECEMBER 2018

Playwright
Peta Tait

Director
Deborah Leiser-Moore

Musician
Adi Sappir

Design
Tashmadada

Lighting Design
Tashmadada

Eleanor Roosevelt – **Sarah McNeill**

Mary Alice Evatt – **Petra Kalive**

Winston Churchill / Franklin D. Roosevelt / Dr Herbert Vere Evatt – **recorded by Richard Moore**

EVATT FOUNDATION

The Evatt Foundation was launched in the Great Hall of the University of Sydney in 1979 as a memorial to Dr Herbert Vere Evatt, with the aim of advancing the highest ideals of the labour movement: equality, democracy, social justice and human rights. A non-profit and independent self-governing democratic body, for almost 40 years the Foundation has pursued these ideals through research, publications, public discussion and debate. In keeping with Dr Evatt's career as a brilliant student, the Foundation is affiliated with the University of Sydney.

TASHMADADA

Tashmadada is a Contemporary Arts Company committed to bringing together practitioners as well as providing a forum for discussion about the arts and current ideas. It collaborates artistically to challenge and cross genres, international borders and mediums. Tashmadada encourages collaboration between artists from different art forms and cultures; connects with new artists; and engages with arts ecology. By creating new works as well as working with existing texts in an original and innovative manner, Tashmadada encourages discussion and engagement through arts practice using theatre and the arts to articulate a multiplicity of voices and cultural traditions.

Eleanor and Mary Alice is about war, human rights and importantly art, and it was first staged at the Heide Museum of Modern Art in a site-specific location at the original house (now gallery Heide 1) that the Evatts visited in 1937. We then reworked it for the Seymour Centre season.

PLAYWRIGHT'S NOTE

Eleanor and Mary Alice is based on the lives of real people and actual events. While this reflects a major trend in theatre, the play comes out of my fascination with these crucial historical events and the realization that these have received minimal attention. A drama with character intentions and tensions, the concerns of these two women contain a number of intriguing resonances that continue today.

Eleanor and Mary Alice expands on earlier drama about asylum seekers but locates the issues in relation to Australia's major contribution in an international context through the work of Herbert Evatt as the first President of the UN General Assembly.

Eleanor's epic flight in 1943 in the middle of the war across the Pacific including to Australia and New Zealand is barely recognized. While Eleanor's life carried the expectations of her era as a wife and mother, it also encompassed additional ones arising from her husband's long leadership of the USA, and during the war, and Eleanor was tireless in her public work on behalf of racial and economic equality.

Left leaning artist and arts broker, Mary Alice contributed to the development of modernism in Australian art, and the regional gallery movement, and provided significant support to Herbert's political contribution during World War II and at the UN. The Evatts advocated that the arts could advance the causes of social equity, education and justice. Broadly, the play depicts how individuals and their friendships influence political events and cultural development.

My sincere thanks to Deborah Leiser-Moore for such an imaginative and moving production of the play and to the wonderful performers, Petra Kalive (and for the play's creative development), Sarah McNeill and Adi Sappir who worked with such sincere commitment and integrity to bring these characters to life.

— Peta Tait

PETA TAIT
PLAYWRIGHT

Peta Tait's *Eleanor and Mary Alice* about Eleanor Roosevelt's meeting with Mary Alice Evatt was first staged in 2014. *Mesmerized*, co-written with Matra Robertson about Charcot and his patient, the hysteric Augustine, was staged in Brazil between 2010 and 2012 with an arts-funded Portuguese translation, *Retrato de Augustine* (Portrait of Augustine). Other plays in the 2000s include: *Deception River*, produced in the 2008 Manawatu One-Act Playwriting Competition, and readings of *Hope Pass*, *Jade Creek* and *S_old*. A graduate of the NIDA Playwrights' Studio, Tait had five short and full-length works staged during the 1980s, and worked as dramatist with the Sydney-based, *The Party Line* during the 1990s on Australia Council-funded performances, *Appearing in Pieces* 1993, and *Whet Flesh* 1998, and on the award-winning *700 Positions* 1996. *Breath by Breath*, co-written with Matra Robertson about asylum seekers, received a 2003 Green Room Award Nomination for best production. She is a Professor of Theatre and Drama at La Trobe University and a widely published author of books and articles, and she was elected to the Australian Academy of the Humanities in 2013.

DEBORAH LEISER-MOORE
DIRECTOR

Deborah is an interdisciplinary performance maker/director who makes bold visceral works. She is equally adept at large scale works or intimate performances, and is known for her visual and physical approach to text. Deborah has toured extensively, notably to New York performing in Richard Schechner's *Imagining O*. In 2017/2018 she worked with Ranters Theatre in collaboration with Korean company, Creative VaQi, in *Unknown Neighbors* at Ansan Festival and as part of Festival of Live Arts at Theatre Works. She presented her solo duration live-art work, *My Body, My Country* at the 2017 Queer Zagreb Festival, Croatia and toured the promenade production of *The Dead Twin*, which she directed and performs in, to George Town Festival in Penang, Malaysia. In 2018 she traveled back to George Town Festival with her performance/installation performance work *KaBooM: Stories From Distant Frontlines* for which she interviewed ex-soldiers form global conflicts (previously presented at fortyfivedownstairs and the Alice Desert Festival in Alice Springs). Deborah is presently working on *M: Kaddish For The Children* – based on both the classic *Euripides* and Heiner Muller's texts of *Medea*, but told from the woman's perspective, intertwined with the Kaddish, the Jewish Mourners Prayer—which will be presented at Footscray Community Arts Centre as part of International Women's Day in 2019. Deborah recently completed her practice led PhD at La Trobe University. More works on her website: www.deborahleisermoore.com

ADI SAPPIR
MUSICIAN

Adi Sappir, a Melbourne-based cellist and vocalist delivers a musical fusion of East meets West. As an Israeli-Australian living in Melbourne, Adi composes lyrical stories reflecting her cultural background and personal experience. She has released three solo albums featuring her unique compositions that are rich and intimate in tone. In recent years Adi has collaborated with various musicians and artists on a number of projects including theatre productions, art exhibitions and literary events and festivals across Australia. She organizes an annual concert in Melbourne to promote cross cultural communication through music. Adi has performed in venues such as the Melbourne Recital Centre, National Gallery of Victoria and Melbourne Museum. She also took part in music festivals such as Port Fairy and Adelaide Fringe Festivals. As an undercurrent in all her projects, Adi continues to create the nostalgic and unique tones she is renowned for.

SARAH MCNEILL
PERFORMER

Perth actor, Sarah McNeill, has performed with Black Swan State Theatre Company, including co-productions with Queensland Theatre and Melbourne Theatre Company; Perth Theatre Company including several national tours, Effie Crump Theatre with state-wide tours, the Civic Theatre restaurant and many independent companies. Television and film credits include the soon-to-be released series, *The Heights*, *The Circuit*, series I and II and the award-winning shorts, *Setting Them Straight* and *You Have Blue Eyes*. Sarah is the producer and presenter of Lit Live Perth, with actors reading short fiction live on stage, and is a regular MC and host for arts and literary events. She is also an arts writer and theatre reviewer for a local Perth newspaper.

PETRA KALIVE
PERFORMER

Petra Kalive trained at the Western Australian Academy of Performing Arts in Acting (2004) and has since been working professionally as an actor, director, dramaturg and facilitator. She is currently Artistic Director of Union House Theatre at Melbourne University Student Union. Petra has extensive experience as an actor, director and dramaturg especially of new works for the stage. Her acclaimed adaptation of Peter Goldsworthy's novel *Three Dog Night* toured nationally in 2009. She was Dramaturg at Red Stitch from 2009–2012, and Assistant Dramaturg at The Malthouse in 2010. At Melbourne Theatre Company she has directed *Hungry Ghosts*, *Melbourne Talam* (Green Room Nom Best Direction), *Beached* (winner of the 2010 Patrick White Award), *In the Kingdom of Cha* (Cybec Electric), and was Assistant Director on *Constellations* and on STC's *Macbeth*. Petra has directed for Arena Theatre Company, Complete Works Theatre Company, St Martins Youth Arts Centre, and in La Trobe and Monash University performing arts programs. Her most recent work as a director includes the much-acclaimed *Taxithi* which played two sell-out seasons at fortyfivedownstairs, *Mirror's Edge* (Patrick White Award Winner 2018) and her own work *Oil Babies* at Northcote Town Hall as part of the Darebin Speak Easy Program.

Tashmadada Theatre gratefully acknowledges the keen interest and vital financial support received from the Evatt Foundation and Gandel Philanthropy, and for making the 2018 production possible.

Peta Tait would like to acknowledge the La Trobe University Social Research Assistance Platform for providing research support to the production of *Eleanor and Mary Alice* in 2018, and to the LTU DPR for research support in 2016 and 2017. Substantial research about Mary Alice Evatt came courtesy of Dr Melissa Boyde. Peta Tait also thanks Amanda Lawson, Matra Robertson, Norie Neumark, Sue Thomas, Annie McGuigan, and Jenny and Jack Tait.

Eleanor and Mary Alice has been endorsed in the three-part program to mark 70 years of the Universal Declaration of Human Rights by Sydney Ideas, United Nations Association of Australia, the ACTU and Amnesty International.

www.currency.com.au

Visit Currency Press' website now to:
- Order books
- Browse through our full list of titles including plays, screenplays, theory and reference/criticism, performance handbooks, educational texts and more
- Choose a play for your school or performance group by cast specs
- Seek performance rights
- Find out about performing arts news and sign up for our newsletter
- For students: read our study guides
- For teachers: access free curriculum information and teacher notes

We are also on Facebook and Instagram (@currencypress). Join the conversation!

The performing arts publisher

www.ingramcontent.com/pod-product-compliance
Lightning Source LLC
Chambersburg PA
CBHW050027090426
42734CB00021B/3448